We are moving to another country
Author: Erica Mirochnik
Illustrations and design: Daniela Wegbrait
Copyright © 2018.
All rights reserved.
Reproduction and distribution in whole or in part
are prohibited without permission.

Index

We are moving to another country 5

The Move 13

My New School 23

Activities 34

Here are Mom and Dad.
Yesterday they told us that
we are going on a kind of adventure together.
That seemed pretty mysterious,
so we wanted to know more!

We are moving to another country 5

"I want to know!" said Gabriel

"What is it?" said Sophia

Mom and Dad told us that we are going to live in another country.

We are moving to another country 6

Dad will have a job in another office, and because it is very far away we are moving to another house.
To go see the house we are going to travel in an airplane because it is in another country, which is not close to home.

We are moving to another country

Mom and Dad answered all our questions.

I don't want to move!

Are there any mountains?

Does it snow?

Are we going on vacation?

When are we leaving?

Are we going for a long time?

We are moving to another country 8

Are Grandma and Grandpa coming with us?

What about the rest of the family?

They are not moving with us, they are staying here, but they will come to visit us and see our new home. It will be really fun!

Are any of my friends coming too?

It is only the four of us, your friends will stay in their homes, with their families, but we will come to visit them very soon.

We are moving to another country 10

Mom and Dad said that we will leave soon, and they will need our help.
We are going to take all our toys and the things that we love.

I want to see the new house!

What a great idea!

We will all be very happy.
We will visit new places, meet new friends and learn new games.
It will be a great adventure.

We are moving to another country 12

The Move

We are moving to another country 13

We are packing our things, putting everything in boxes.
The house feels different.

We are moving to another country 14

Mom said that it will be fun to put our favorite books and toys in the boxes. We can choose what we want to bring and we can color and decorate our own box!

We are moving to another country

A new house is waiting for us. I am sure you will love it!
We will put all your games in your new room.

What a great idea!

We are moving to another country 16

But we will not have friends to play with…

I am sure you will meet new friends soon.
They will love to get to know you and have playdates with you.

We are moving to another country 17

Do you think I will like my new school?

I am sure you will!
You will learn so many interesting things

We are moving to another country 18

The day has come to say goodbye.
We are going to the airport where we will
board a plane that will take us to our new home.

We are moving to another country 19

We have the passports.

We have the suitcases!

I love planes!

0246	BUENOS AIRES	ON TIME
214	SANTIAGO	DELAYED
764	MADRID	LANDED
003	NEW YORK	LANDED
753	MONTREAL	DELAYED
211	PARIS	ON TIME
452	LA PAZ	ON TIME
900	QUITO	DELAYED

We are moving to another country 20

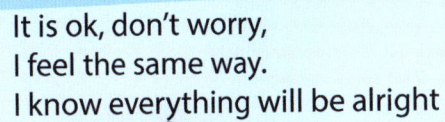

I feel weird,
I don't know if I am happy or sad…

It is ok, don't worry,
I feel the same way.
I know everything will be alright

We are moving to another country

We are ready for take off! It is great to fly!

We are moving to another country 22

My New School

We are moving to another country 23

Today is the first day at a new school. Sophia and Gabriel want to meet their new friends, and they feel pretty nervous about it.

I think it will be too hard for me.

Do you think I will like it?

I think we are ready. It will be a great day!

We are moving to another country.

I see how anxious you feel about meeting your new friends.

Yes, I am! I want to meet them and start playing with them.

Do you think I will have a nice teacher?

I am sure about it! You will see, she will help you if you need her.

We are moving to another country 25

The parents and kids say goodbye.
They will see each other when school ends
and share all that happened on the first day.

I will be waiting to hear all about your new school
when I get back from work.

Bye! See you after school!

We are moving to another country 26

Sophia thinks …
It can't be too hard, I am sure it will be ok.
The kids seem nice,
we will become friends very soon.

We are moving to another country 27

A E I O U

The classroom looks really nice!
there are a lot of toys.
I am not sure which one to choose!

We are moving to another country

Gabriel pays attention but he doesn´t understand what the teacher is saying.

I think she wants me to draw with markers and colored pencils.

We are moving to another country

When school ends, Mom is waiting for them at the door.

Sophia, Gabriel, I am here!

We are moving to another country 30

Who wants to start?

The school is really big. The teacher is nice and my new friends asked a lot of questions!

It was a good day, some kids wanted to play with me.

We are moving to another country 31

You will have new friends really soon. The language seems hard but you will learn it easily. You already know so many words! The best way to learn is to ask for help from teachers and friends.

The End

Color

Color

```
P L A N E G E A R
F S I O N T E C E
T C M I B O X E S
R F R I E N D S A
I S C H O O L J E
P O C U E L I T E
F A M I L Y R I P
```

Find the words:
Plane - Boxes - Family - School - Trip - Friends

PASSPORT

Your photo here

Type

Last name

Name

Birthplace

Birth date

Gender

Valid since

Passport number

Valid until

Signature

Fill your passport

Draw and color

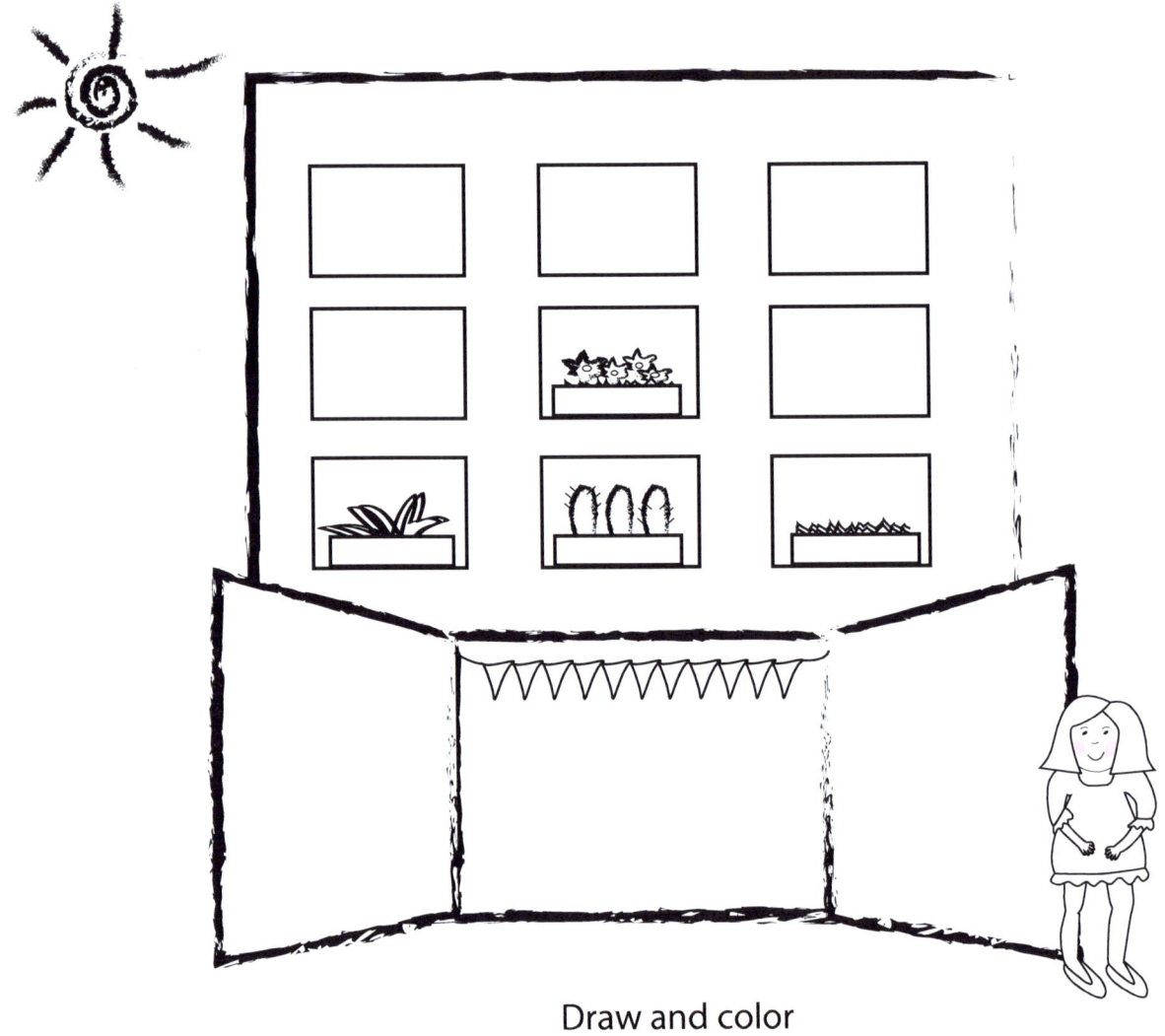

Color

My New Friends

My School

My New Teachers

Printed by Amazon Italia Logistica S.r.l.
Torrazza Piemonte (TO), Italy